Creating and Maintaining Effective Local Government Citizen Advisory Committees

Vaughn M. Upshaw

Access an Electronic Version of the Model Policy and Tracking Forms

Purchase of this book includes a FREE electronic version of the model policy and tracking forms that can be customized to fit a particular committee's specific needs.

Visit the following URL to access and download the file in ZIP format: **sog.unc.edu/pubs/9781560116578**

For information about other publications and resources from the School of Government, visit **sog.unc.edu**.

Electronic download available

UNC
SCHOOL OF
GOVERNMENT

The School of Government at the University of North Carolina at Chapel Hill works to improve the lives of North Carolinians by engaging in practical scholarship that helps public officials and citizens understand and improve state and local government. Established in 1931 as the Institute of Government, the School provides educational, advisory, and research services for state and local governments. The School of Government is also home to a nationally ranked graduate program in public administration and specialized centers focused on information technology, environmental finance, and civic education for youth.

As the largest university-based local government training, advisory, and research organization in the United States, the School of Government offers up to 200 courses, seminars, and specialized conferences for more than 12,000 public officials each year. In addition, faculty members annually publish approximately fifty books, book chapters, bulletins, and other reference works related to state and local government. Each day that the General Assembly is in session, the School produces the *Daily Bulletin*, which reports on the day's activities for members of the legislature and others who need to follow the course of legislation.

The Master of Public Administration Program is a full-time, two-year program that serves up to sixty students annually. It consistently ranks among the best public administration graduate programs in the country, particularly in city management. With courses ranging from public policy analysis to ethics and management, the program educates leaders for local, state, and federal governments and nonprofit organizations.

Operating support for the School of Government's programs and activities comes from many sources, including state appropriations, local government membership dues, private contributions, publication sales, course fees, and service contracts. Visit www.sog.unc.edu or call 919.966.5381 for more information on the School's courses, publications, programs, and services.

Michael R. Smith, DEAN
Thomas H. Thornburg, SENIOR ASSOCIATE DEAN
Frayda S. Bluestein, ASSOCIATE DEAN FOR FACULTY DEVELOPMENT
Todd A. Nicolet, ASSOCIATE DEAN FOR OPERATIONS
Ann Cary Simpson, ASSOCIATE DEAN FOR DEVELOPMENT AND COMMUNICATIONS
Bradley G. Volk, ASSOCIATE DEAN FOR ADMINISTRATION

FACULTY

Gregory S. Allison
David N. Ammons
Ann M. Anderson
A. Fleming Bell, II
Maureen M. Berner
Mark F. Botts
Michael Crowell
Shea Riggsbee Denning
James C. Drennan
Richard D. Ducker
Joseph S. Ferrell
Alyson A. Grine

Norma Houston (on leave)
Cheryl Daniels Howell
Jeffrey A. Hughes
Willow S. Jacobson
Robert P. Joyce
Kenneth L. Joyner
Diane M. Juffras
Dona G. Lewandowski
James M. Markham
Janet Mason
Christopher B. McLaughlin
Laurie L. Mesibov

Kara A. Millonzi
Jill D. Moore
Jonathan Q. Morgan
Ricardo S. Morse
C. Tyler Mulligan
David W. Owens
William C. Rivenbark
Dale J. Roenigk
John Rubin
John L. Saxon
Jessica Smith
Karl W. Smith

Carl W. Stenberg III
John B. Stephens
Charles Szypszak
Shannon H. Tufts
Vaughn Upshaw
Aimee N. Wall
Jeffrey B. Welty
Richard B. Whisnant
Gordon P. Whitaker
Eileen R. Youens

Printed in the United States of America
21 20 19 18 17   2 3 4 5 6
ISBN 978-1-56011-657-8

About the Series

Local Government Board Builders offers local elected leaders practical advice on how to effectively lead and govern. Each of the booklets in this series provides a topic overview, specific tips on effective practice, and worksheets and reflection questions to help local elected leaders improve their work. The series focuses on common activities for local governing boards, such as selecting and appointing committees and advisory boards, planning for the future, making better decisions, improving board accountability, and effectively engaging stakeholders in public decisions.

Vaughn Mamlin Upshaw, lecturer in public administration and government at the UNC School of Government, is the series editor.

Other Books in the Series

Leading Your Governing Board: A Guide for Mayors and County Board Chairs, Vaughn Mamlin Upshaw, 2009

A Model Code of Ethics for North Carolina Local Elected Officials, A. Fleming Bell, II, 2010

Working with Nonprofit Organizations, Margaret Henderson, Lydian Altman, Suzanne Julian, Gordon P. Whitaker, and Eileen Youens, forthcoming in 2010

Public Outreach and Participation, John B. Stephens, Ricardo S. Morse, and Kelley T. O'Brien, forthcoming in 2010

Contents

Introduction

Local governments often use appointed policy boards or citizen advisory committees (CACs) to engage people in the democratic process.[1] They may voluntarily establish CACs to support their work or to respond to community-generated issues. These local boards and committees help identify issues and priorities, consider and recommend actions, and evaluate outcomes. Despite the widespread use of CACs, however, developing and integrating their work into the governmental process remains challenging for many local governments.

How can local governments successfully work with advisory boards and committees? This book presents guidelines for local policy boards and advisory committees. It also offers tips on how to evaluate CAC benefits and costs, suggests ways for assessing whether or not to establish a CAC, and provides a model policy.

Types of City and County Advisory Boards and Committees

Virtually all local governments are either required or empowered to appoint advisory committees.[2] Nationally, there is evidence that local governments are expanding their use of citizen advisory committees to help with quasi-legislative and quasi-judicial functions, such as community planning and dispute resolution.[3] In North Carolina, county and municipal leaders appoint citizens to serve on a variety of mandated and optional policy boards and advisory committees. State law requires local governments to establish certain policy boards automatically, and it sets forth conditions that trigger the establishment of others. For example, the general statutes require counties to establish boards for health,[4] social services,[5] and mental health.[6] And as cities adopt certain rules or begin providing certain services, they are required to create advisory boards for planning, adjustment, historic preservation, alcoholic beverage control, and other purposes. However, most citizen advisory committees at the local level are optional and are created to advise city and county leaders on issues such as land use, recreation, environmental protection, transportation, and economic development. City and county governing boards in North Carolina are authorized to establish and appoint citizens to local policy and advisory boards under one or more of the structures shown in Table 1 (see page 5).

The types of citizen advisory committees established at the local level can differ from county to county and city to city. Local elected officials and public administrators have tremendous discretion in deciding what types of CACs to establish. They are also in the best position to assess whether the county's or city's CACs are operating effectively and making a positive contribution to the local government and the community at large.

The following worksheet can be used to identify and record information about local government CACs. Appendix A provides a sample tracking chart.

WORKSHEET: *Identifying CACs and Recording Information*

List your city's or county's statutory boards, citizen advisory committees, and external boards, then ask the following questions:

When was each created?

_____

_____

_____

What powers were granted to it?

_____

_____

_____

Who serves on the board or committee?

_____

_____

_____

For each board or committee, create a list that includes the following information:

- Name of CAC
- Names of members
- Seat each member fills (if seats are designated)
- Vacancies (if any)
- Contact information for each member
- Date of appointment for each member
- Expiration of term
- Eligibility for reappointment (if appropriate)

**Table 1. Local Government's Power and Role
in Establishing Policy Boards and Advisory Committees**

Types of Local Policy Boards and Advisory Committees, with Examples	Local Governing Board Power	Local Governing Board Role
Statutorily Mandated: Board of Public Health Board of Social Services Local Management Entity/ Area Mental Health Authority Health and Human Service Boards	Limited	Establish mandated boards as directed by state law Appoint members as directed by statute Enact local policies covering matters such as when appointments will be made, how reimbursements will be handled
Statutorily Optional: Planning Adjustment Historic Preservation Alcoholic Beverage Commission Housing Authority Water and Sewer Authority	Moderate	Establish at the local level *if* certain conditions are met Appoint members Membership criteria *may* be set by state law Policy and/or rule making authority granted by state law
External Advisory: Council of Governments Community College Board of Trustees[a] Regional Transportation Authority Regional Water or Sewer Authority	Moderate	Appoint local representatives as directed by external entity Authority established by state statute or by external entity Membership criteria set by state law or external entity
Standing Advisory: Parks and Recreation Appearance Library Cemetery Greenway Committee	High	Optional at the local level Governing board establishes by adopting a local policy or ordinance Membership determined by local policy Appoints members Oversight and advisory authority granted by local elected officials
Ad Hoc Advisory: Small Area Land Use Plan Budget Review Festival Planning Committee	High	Optional at the local level Governing board establishes by adopting a local policy or ordinance Membership determined by local policy Appoints members Advisory role granted by local elected officials

[a] Section 115D-12 of the North Carolina General Statutes. Each institution to have board of trustees; selection of trustees. Available at www.ncga.state.nc.us/enactedlegislation/statutes/html/bysection/chapter_115d/gs_115d-12.html.

Reasons for Having Citizen Advisory Committees

When communities face complex issues affecting large, diverse groups, citizen engagement leads to people being better informed, better able to collaborate with others, and more active in addressing issues that affect them.[7] By sharing responsibility, local officials increase opportunities for citizens to contribute to the common good.[8]

At the local level, CACs provide an effective mechanism for program planning and assessment by identifying community needs and interests and soliciting recommendations on how to meet those needs.[9] Local elected and appointed officials may become focused on their own priorities and work, losing sight of larger community concerns.

Certain statutory mandates ensure that interest groups and community representatives have formal input on local government initiatives. Membership criteria that focus on technical and professional experience result in representatives whose interests align with organizational concerns. Technical and professional boards can help local governments plan services *for* particular groups. Membership criteria that require community members, consumers of services, and affected groups to be involved result in citizens having an opportunity to shape services that are important to them. Appointed boards enable citizens to plan *with* local governments. Depending upon what a local government or community seeks to accomplish, citizens can often contribute to the process and provide local government leaders with valuable information.

Tips for Understanding How and Why Your Local Government Uses CACs

Review enabling documents (bylaws, statutes, policies) for local CACs, and ask the following questions:

How clear are the purposes and expectations for each CAC?

_____

_____

_____

Are these articulated in bylaws or other enabling documents?

_____

_____

_____

Spend time as a governing board deciding what the purpose of a CAC should and should not be, and ask the following question:

When does our local government most effectively engage CACs?

_____

_____

_____

Consider how CAC membership invites or restricts the interests of affected communities, private interest groups, and local government, and ask the following questions:

Which of our CACs are designed to plan services *for* others?

_____

_____

_____

Which of our CACs are designed to plan services *with* others?

_____

_____

_____

Discuss the power delegated to local CACs and how effectively they exercise it, and ask the following questions:

What authority is granted to CACs by state law?

_____

_____

_____

What authority is granted to CACs by local policy?

_____

_____

_____

Consider whether CACs provide broader perspectives to elected officials—and, if so, how that helps with decision making—and ask the following questions:

How representative are CAC members of the broader community?

_____

_____

_____

What new or alternative ideas do CACs bring to local government?

_____

_____

_____

Benefits and Costs of Citizen Advisory Committees

Arguments for citizen engagement are strongly rooted in the United States' political culture. Civic engagement is valued for bringing greater public voice into governmental decision making and improving public perceptions of government.[10] Local governments seeking public involvement in governmental decisions often turn to CACs as a way to include citizens in the process. Establishing CACs can benefit local government and the public by providing more ideas and creating more support for decisions. Citizen advisory committees are not without their costs to local governments or the public, though, especially when the issues are complex and defy easy answers.[11]

Benefits to Local Governments

Local governments benefit from CACs by

- *Tapping into the expertise of the citizenry as subject matter experts.* Often people who have extensive experience and knowledge in a particular area (for example, engineering or technology) are interested in using their skills to help improve the communities where they live.
- *Engaging citizens as partners in the process of governing the city or county.* To effectively accomplish community goals, local elected officials routinely work with individual citizens, business and nonprofit leaders, community groups, and other state, regional, and national organizations and governments. Involving key stakeholders in CACs can help move issues forward, because citizens have a role in reviewing alternatives and making recommendations to the local governing board.
- *Gathering information for governing and decision making.* Public problems are rarely straightforward, and few issues have one right answer. Citizens "enlarge the room" by bringing diverse opinions and perspectives to community issues. Citizen

advisory committees are a convenient way to engage representatives with different perspectives in local governance.

- *Making the governing process more transparent.* Many citizens know little about what local government does and have had little experience working with local government. Serving on an advisory board helps citizens learn more about local government issues, challenges, and complexities.

- *Going beyond what they can accomplish alone.* Local governments are expected to address multiple issues simultaneously, and CACs help extend their reach. Citizens often have direct knowledge of resources, partners, and strategies outside of local government. By engaging citizens in CACs, local governments tap into resources that they might not have known about or had access to otherwise.

- *Improving communication between elected officials and the public.* When elected officials participate in advisory boards, either as liaisons or as representatives of the governing board, they interact directly with citizens about community issues. Citizens serving on CACs generally have opportunities to present information or meet directly with elected officials.

- *Receiving new information and perspectives.* Citizens often have information relevant to public issues—as direct consumers of local government services, as representatives of community organizations, or as professionals with relevant expertise. Better decisions result when decision makers consider and weigh multiple points of view.

- *Linking to other resources and groups interested in addressing community issues.* Through their work on advisory boards, citizens can network and collaborate with others.

- *Reducing the likelihood that government decisions will be challenged in court.* When citizens have a chance to participate in the decision making process, they better understand the trade-offs among competing options and are less likely to sue their local governments when the final decision is not their first preference.

- *Expanding citizens' understanding of how local government works.* Citizens may have limited experience working with local government. When citizens serve on CACs, government officials can communicate with them about particular issues in the context of the local government's broader responsibilities.

> **Advantages of CACS: A Case Example**
>
> **A Historic Preservation Committee Helps Local
> Government Achieve Multiple Community Goals**
>
> Community groups, individuals, local businesses, and historic property owners recommend priorities and alternatives for revitalization and provide expertise on historic preservation to local government staff. Committee members routinely communicate with local government officials and other community groups, such as the local economic development committee and the tourism commission, about how historic preservation contributes to larger community goals.

Benefits to Citizens

Citizens benefit from CACs by

- *Learning about local government and opportunities for future leadership.* Advisory boards are a vehicle for developing citizens' leadership capacity. Learning about and dealing with public issues helps citizens better understand the roles and responsibilities of local government. Advisory board members who later run for office may appreciate a city's or county's role more than citizens unfamiliar with the workings of local government.

- *Understanding and becoming more trusting of local government.* Advisory board members have an opportunity to work with other citizens, elected officials, and local government employees. Working with others promotes understanding and trust.

- *Having a greater stake and more investment in the outcome of decisions.* Advisory board members engaged in reviewing alternatives are more likely to support final decisions than are citizens who have not been involved in looking at multiple options.

- *Being directly involved in finding solutions.* An individual who is concerned about services or policies can speak directly to public officials or address the governing board at public hearings. Citizen concerns are often too extensive for an elected board to address quickly. Advisory boards provide citizens a more focused forum in which to raise concerns and express interests.

> **Challenges of CACs: A Case Example**
>
> **A Local Governing Board Establishes a Review Committee to
> Provide Ideas about Future Development in a Specific Area**
>
> Citizens volunteer to serve on the committee, and the group is all white and mostly male. At the first meeting, a member volunteers to be the chair and others agree. Soon it becomes clear that the chair has a personal interest in how a nearby area will be developed. Staff attempt to redirect the group's attention to the main goal and offer alternate perspectives on how to proceed, but they are overruled by the chair. The CAC supports the chair's recommendations on how local government should approach development, but it fails to make recommendations for the specific area under review by the governing board. The governing board accepts the committee's recommendations then directs staff to perform a review of the area under consideration. The chair of the CAC writes an angry letter to the editor of the local newspaper accusing the governing board of ignoring citizen input and pursuing personal agendas.

Costs for Local Governments

For local governments, some of the costs of having CACs occur when

- *The CAC is time consuming for local government staff.* Recruiting and selecting members and providing support for CACs can require a lot of time on the part of local elected officials and local government staff.

- *The CAC is costly to support.* The financial costs of supporting some CAC work can be considerable, particularly if the issue requires detailed input from external technical advisors and substantial staff time to research and prepare reports.

- *Involving the public in a CAC creates tension or hostility.* If members of the public think that local government is trying to force an agenda through the CAC, or if the group itself is divided and dysfunctional, dissatisfaction can set in. This can result in disenchantment on the part of the CAC members, criticism of the local government's process, and hostility toward the local government rather than support for the issue.

- *Local government loses control over decision making.* If the governing board has not set clear boundaries, a CAC can assume more authority than was intended. Unless the local governing board is willing to rein in the CAC, the group may make decisions and pursue options without local government's full support.

- *The CAC makes bad recommendations.* If the CAC is made up of people with similar views, the committee may limit input or introduce data from unreliable sources to influence the process. Or, if members of the CAC cannot get along and work together, members may not agree on recommendations. In either case, the outcome is likely to result in a flawed decision for local government.

- *There is inadequate communication.* Limited interaction between the CAC and elected officials can lead to elected officials being unaware of CAC activities or, worse, working at cross-purposes with the CAC. Unless elected officials serve as liaisons to CACs or a regular process is established for sharing information with the governing board, the CAC (and support staff) can move forward with proposals and/or recommendations without elected officials understanding what they are doing.

Costs for Citizens

For citizens, some of the costs of serving on CACs occur when

- *Participation on CACs is time consuming.* Depending upon the issue, the CAC may meet quarterly, monthly, bimonthly, or even weekly. Citizens who are deeply involved in an issue may participate in meetings outside of the CAC as well. For many members of the public, the time commitment required to serve on a CAC can be a deterrent to participation.
- *The CAC has poorly defined objectives.* Unclear expectations, goals that are too broad, or timelines that are unreasonable lead to groups floundering for focus. In some cases, CACs will create their own goals and objectives if they believe they do not have sufficient guidance from elected officials. If the group's goals are in conflict with the intent of the elected board, the process may be fraught with conflict.
- *The process for the CAC is flawed.* If the path to achieving results is cumbersome or confusing, if members have unresolved conflicts, if leadership changes too often or not often enough, or if insufficient resources are allocated to the CAC, members and interest groups may become dissatisfied with both the CAC and local government.
- *Needed expertise is unavailable within the CAC.* Complex public issues often require specialized knowledge beyond what the average citizen possesses. When CACs are established to recommend or review local government actions but no member of the CAC understands the issue well enough to provide an informed opinion, the task is likely to be overwhelming and frustrating.
- *Interest groups dominate the process and do not represent the broader interests of the community.* Vocal advocates for and opponents of an issue often seek seats on CACs. Unless the process used to appoint members to a CAC assures a mix of perspectives, citizens will reject the outcomes because their voices are unrepresented or underrepresented.

- *Recommendations and advice are not adopted.* Citizens who spend significant time learning about an issue and preparing recommendations may be frustrated if their recommendations are not embraced by elected officials or public administrators.

When benefits are high and costs are low, the conditions for establishing a CAC are more favorable. Less favorable conditions occur when the benefits of establishing a CAC are low and the costs of doing so are high.

The following tips can help local governments increase benefits and reduce costs associated with CACs.

Tips for Increasing Benefits and Decreasing Costs

- Ensure that advisory board members, elected officials, and staff members have similar—if not the same—expectations about the goals of the CAC.
- Assess the contribution of CACs to local government. Consider dissolving or changing CACs that have outlived their usefulness.
- Annually review CAC purposes and revise, as needed, each CAC's focus and expectations.
- Require all CACs to operate openly and provide opportunities for citizen input and comment.
- Make sure staff members understand how to use CACs to increase options and potential strategies for success.
- Meet regularly with each CAC to share information and develop a partnership to accomplish community goals.
- Establish common templates for CAC reports and minutes, making it easier for decision makers to oversee progress on stated priorities.
- Periodically convene all CACs and the governing board to engage in "big picture" thinking about the community, giving everyone a chance to see and hear different perspectives on issues affecting the community's future.
- Hold an annual event to recognize and reward CAC members for their contributions.
- When a CAC has completed its work, celebrate the achievement and then dissolve the group.

The following worksheet can be used by local governments to identify the benefits and costs of CACs, both for the local government and for community members.

WORKSHEET: *Identifying Benefits and Costs*

For local government:

What are the benefits of having CACs?

_____

_____

_____

What are the costs or challenges of having CACs?

_____

_____

_____

How do the benefits compare to the costs?

_____

_____

_____

For community members:

What motivates people to serve on CACs?

_____

_____

_____

Why do community members resist serving on CACs?

_____

_____

_____

How do community members describe the benefits and costs of serving on CACs?

_____

_____

_____

Deciding to Establish a
Citizen Advisory Committee

Except when boards are mandated by law, local elected officials have to decide for themselves whether or not to create CACs. Local officials may gather citizen input in a variety of ways, some of which do not require CACs. For example, they can hold focus groups, conduct community surveys, or hire external consultants to poll the community. When the governing board decides to establish a CAC, it needs to take into account the community's history of participation and design a process that fits the community's culture and experience with local government.[12]

A citizen advisory committee may be needed to help a local government address longstanding issues or make recommendations for a particular project. Most CACs are ad hoc committees that focus on a particular issue for a specified period of time, make their reports, and are then dissolved.[13] Some CACs, however, are standing committees that make recommendations to county or city governing boards on issues of ongoing importance to the community. Both standing and ad hoc CACs may consider expert advice, review alternatives, and agree on recommendations to the governing board. The final decision, however, always remains in the hands of the county or city governing board.

Local governments should carefully consider whether they genuinely want public participation on particular issues. They have the option of engaging citizens in a variety of ways (see Appendix B, the IAP2 Spectrum of Participation), and no one approach is best in every situation. Sometimes local decision makers just want to see where the majority of community members stand on an issue, and a simple survey will suffice. Citizen advisory committees, advisory boards, and policy forums, on the other hand, offer diverse stakeholders an opportunity to exchange information and shape opinions on complex public issues over time.[14] Public participation through CACs is preferable when local governments need citizen input and public support for the proposed solution.

When deciding to create a CAC, local elected officials should consider the following:[15]

- *Process.* What type of CAC (standing or ad hoc) will be used under which circumstances? Is there flexibility to change the type of CAC if necessary? How might the type of CAC influence the group's work and outcomes?

- *Timing.* At what point(s) in the local government decision making process is a CAC needed, and how can its input be used most effectively? Will the work of the CAC be completed in time to contribute to the decision making process?
- *Logistics.* Where will meetings be held? Is the local government responsible for providing meeting space?
- *Support.* What level of staff support will the CAC require? What management support is needed to integrate the work of the CAC into the broader work of the local government? How much support can local government staff provide? What other options are available to support the CAC's work?
- *Cost.* What will it cost to support the work of the CAC? Have these costs been budgeted? How much cost is local government willing to bear to support the CAC?
- *Representation.* How can equal representation and balance be achieved? How will people be recruited? What skills and knowledge do people need to bring to the table? How will diversity and inclusion be handled? How will people be oriented to their roles and responsibilities? How will trust and good working relationships among participants be cultivated?
- *Policy.* What information will CACs provide to decision makers? What will be the process for communicating with decision makers? At what point(s) in the policy making process will information be provided?
- *Outcomes.* What is the purpose of the CAC and what are the expected outcomes? Are the goals clearly defined? What measurements will be used to assess progress? Are desired outcomes the same for different stakeholders? Have expectations been mutually created so that they address the interests of CAC members and local government officials? How will CAC work contribute to better local government outcomes? Have these outcomes been clearly articulated, and do citizens and key stakeholders agree on them?
- *Implementation.* Will elected officials, citizens, or staff provide leadership for the CAC? Will CAC leaders be appointed by the governing board or elected by vote of the CAC members? How will local elected officials interact with or be involved with the CAC?
- *Institutionalization.* Are there things the local government needs to keep doing after an ad hoc CAC has completed its work? Are there CACs that need to be discontinued? What CAC goals have been accomplished? Who has responsibility for reviewing the success of CACs, and how often does this occur? What is the process local government will use for reviewing, modifying, continuing, or eliminating CACs?

Table 2. Benefits and Costs of Establishing Citizen Advisory Committees (CACs) under More Favorable and Less Favorable Conditions

	More Favorable Conditions	Less Favorable Conditions
Benefits	(more benefits)	(fewer benefits)
	Issue is gridlocked and citizens are needed to move policy and government leaders ahead	Public trusts government to implement policy or program
	Citizens bring useful knowledge and skills	Local government has success without citizen participation
	Influential community representatives are willing to get involved	Large, diverse population makes representation hard to achieve
	CAC chair/facilitator is seen as credible by all parties	CAC decisions unlikely to be used by decision and policy makers
	Issue is of high interest to participants and they agree to need for change	CAC decisions likely to differ from local government's existing plans and preferences
Costs	(fewer costs)	(more costs)
	Citizens eager to volunteer for CAC	Citizens reluctant to do government's job
	Key stakeholders can easily participate face-to-face	Geography makes face-to-face meetings difficult
	Citizens are provided sufficient resources to participate	People with limited resources unable to participate
	Fewer interest groups have a stake, small group can do the work	Multiple, competing interests and large group
	Topic is something citizens can understand (not too technical)	Complex technical knowledge is needed to address issue
	Public perceives issue as critical	Public does not perceive issue as important

Local officials need to keep in mind the ways in which citizens view an issue within the community. Do people really want to get involved in a certain issue, or are they willing to let government implement a solution? Some issues are divisive and people feel strongly about having a say in how decisions are made. Other issues are less divisive and citizens may be content to let government resolve them. Table 2 sets out the benefits and costs of establishing CACs under more favorable and less favorable conditions.[16]

Recruitment and Selection of Members

State-mandated policy boards and standing CACs usually rotate members on an annual or biannual basis, making it difficult to retain people who are committed to each other, local government, or community causes. Unless they are thoughtfully structured, CACs can relegate interest group representatives to a marginal role and undermine citizens' trust in local government.[17]

Perhaps the biggest challenge for local governments that want to establish productive and effective CACs is attracting the right people from the beginning.[18] Local officials are faced with the challenge of setting CAC membership criteria and recruiting and selecting citizens who are interested in the issue, are able to work well with others, have a commitment to community activities, and are able to attend face-to-face meetings for a period of time (often months or even years).

Selecting people with the right mix of skills is critical to a CAC's success, but it is often hard to get people to agree to serve on CACs. If local governments need to address issues affecting diverse groups within the community and local government leaders find it challenging to engage diverse representatives in CACs, they may need to allocate additional resources to help those who do participate remain fully involved. Results of studies examining citizen participation on citizen advisory committees suggest that participants are more likely to be "better educated, higher income, white, and more politically active . . . [and] not at all representative of the wider public."[19] As they consider goals for the CAC, local elected leaders can discuss what mix of community influence, technical expertise, personal experience, and professional interest will be needed to accomplish the task at hand.

It takes time to identify a diverse, representative group of citizens able to collaborate in situations where they disagree. To ensure productive, effective CACs, those involved in the selection process need to "treat appointment decisions as personnel decisions and with the same interest and concerns used to hire full-time staff."[20] Depending upon the number of CACs at the local level, public officials can spend a substantial amount of time recruiting and selecting citizens to serve. Using a selection matrix can help local officials identify key groups that need to be involved in a CAC or evaluate membership gaps on existing CACs (see Appendix C). Developing a standard and straightforward application process for CAC membership helps ensure that the same information is collected on all applicants. Providing information about CAC activities and vacancies and distributing copies of the application throughout the community can increase the range of potential participants.

There are three common biases that public administrators and elected officials need to be aware of when selecting members for an advisory board or committee:[21]

- *Education.* Educated people are more likely to be asked to serve on CACs. There is a perception among public administrators that people with more education will make better decisions and recommendations. For complex, technical issues, public administrators and elected officials lean toward appointing better educated citizens because such participants are thought to lower the risk of lawsuits against local governments.
- *Marketing.* Public administrators and elected officials may see the CAC as a tool for local government to sway citizens toward a particular point of view. Local elected officials and public administrators may seek out citizens to serve on CACs because the committee members are seen as ambassadors or champions for local government initiatives within their communities.
- *Reflection.* Public administrators and elected officials are comfortable working with people who look like them and act as they do. They are also more likely to invite persons with whom they are already acquainted to serve on CACs. Elected and appointed officials therefore need to ask themselves, "What voices are not being heard?" and then work to bring into the room the voices that are missing.

Tips for Successfully Recruiting and Selecting CAC Members

An inclusive selection process is a vital part of creating a successful CAC. The following strategies are associated with successful CACs:[22]

- *Having a fair and transparent formula for balancing community representation on the CAC (race, age, socioeconomic status, geographic location, etc.).* Publicize criteria for membership so the community knows who will be represented.
- *Creating a "culture of welcome" so that all participants feel accepted.* Make sure the neighborhood resident feels as respected and important to the CAC as the business leader.
- *Selecting members who are trusted to represent the interests of others in their communities and networks.* Sometimes, the first people to volunteer for a CAC have

a personal stake in an issue that differs from what members of the larger community want. Selecting people who are trusted members of the community will increase the likelihood that a wide range of citizens will accept the CAC's process and the outcome.

- *Clarifying the CAC's purpose and the limits to its authority.* If the CAC is established to make recommendations on a specific issue, be clear about what that issue does and does not include. For example, a CAC might be charged with reviewing and advising the governing board on downtown development, but only within a specified three-block area.

- *Building CAC members' skills to enable them to interact effectively with other members of the group.* As new members are appointed, provide the CAC with basic guidance on how to work well together, how to have effective meetings, and how to operate openly.

- *Engaging participants in such a way that they bring credible and relevant information to the process.* Give CAC members tasks that they can realistically accomplish, that take advantage of their knowledge and networks, and that contribute to accomplishing the overall goal.

- *Developing a standard application for CAC membership.* Provide applicants with a brief description of the CAC's purpose and goals along with the application and include a statement of expectations for CAC members so that people understand what they are signing up for.

- *Reviewing vacancies and expiring terms on a monthly basis.* Track vacancies to determine how long seats remain open. When seats remain open for extended periods of time, consider redesigning the membership and goals of the CAC or eliminating it if it is no longer useful.

- *Distributing information about CACs and vacancies widely in the community.* Invite citizens to join CACs through local newspapers, listservs, government websites, local radio and television public service announcements, and community events.

A local government should consider the following questions when establishing a process to select and appoint CAC members:

1. How are people selected to serve on CACs? What approaches have worked well in your experience? What have not worked well?
2. What extra efforts are needed to get women, young people, clients, people of color, and other underrepresented groups to participate? How will these participants be supported so that they can be productive members of the CAC?

3. How will the local government determine whether people are (1) interested in the issues the CAC is to address; (2) committed to serve the community, not themselves; and (3) able to create a culture of openness and collaboration rather than an elite club for a chosen few?

4. What information will be made available to potential candidates in advance so that they can assess their interest in being a part of the group and working toward its goals? What will be done to help people understand their roles and responsibilities as members of the CAC?

5. Once CAC members are selected, what will be done to ensure that they receive a standard orientation? For instance, will CAC members receive information about open meetings and public records laws? Will they be instructed in what the CAC is and is not authorized to do?

6. How will leadership be determined? Will a leader be designated by the appointing authority or will the CAC members determine whom their leader will be?

7. How long will members serve on the CAC? What will be the process for reappointing members to the CAC? How many consecutive terms can they serve?

Thinking through the questions on the following worksheet before selecting CAC members can help make the recruitment process run more smoothly. And many potential CAC members will also want answers to questions such as these before they agree to serve.[23]

WORKSHEET: *Defining Mutual Expectations between a County/ City Governing Board and a Citizen Advisory Committee*

1. What is the overall purpose of this relationship?

2. What specifically do you hope to accomplish by having this relationship? Consider benefits for both members of the group and any stakeholders outside the group.

- Communication
- Interaction
- Tasks
- Events
- Products
- Processes
- Other outcomes

3. Who can or should participate regularly in this group's meetings?

- Are there others who can or should *periodically* participate in meetings or provide feedback to guide the actions of this group?
- Will leadership roles be assigned or rotated?
- Who can bring issues to the group's attention through either the formal agenda or informal discussion?

4. Who is expected to carry out which actions, and for whom?

- Logistical arrangements for convening meetings
- Financial management
- Communicating with group members or external stakeholders
- Implementing new or revised service or support activities

5. Who can invoke or alter these expectations? Under what circumstances?

6. How will decisions be made within the group?

- About the group's procedures and selection of officers
- About the group's finances
- About the group's service population or desired outcomes
- About the group's joint or coordinated service or support activities

7. How will resources be shared or allocated?

8. How will the group report on its activities, responsibilities, or progress?

- Content and format of information
- Who receives the information
- Who reports the information to whom
- How this information can be used outside the group

9. How will the group evaluate its success?

Designing an Advisory Board Policy

The specifics of a CAC policy will vary depending upon the type of CAC being established. Even so, good CAC policies will contain many common components. The model components presented below include sections that might be included in a policy establishing a CAC, but every section may not be appropriate for a particular CAC.

If there are standard policies that apply to all or most CACs, a city or county may choose to adopt a generic policy covering all standard practices. It may then develop shorter, more specific policies for individual CACs, with references to the generic CAC policy as appropriate. Appendix D is a template for a policy that could be modified to work for a variety of CACs.

A CAC policy should have some or all of the following components:

1. *Scope*

The first section of a CAC policy broadly outlines the scope and purpose of the CAC being established. This section also asserts the governing board's authority to create the CAC and designates a timetable for reviewing the CAC and the policy.

2. *Duties*

Under this section, a CAC policy more specifically describes the CAC's goals and expected results. This section might also include a statement describing the role of the CAC as an extension of local government and emphasizing members' duties to represent the CAC appropriately in the community.

3. *Membership*

This section sets forth the criteria that will be used to determine whether an individual is eligible to serve on a CAC. It also establishes how many appointments there will be and who will make those appointments; clarifies the length of each term and the number of terms a member can serve; and outlines procedures for handling vacancies, removing members, and naming replacements.

4. *Roles and Responsibilities*

Expectations for individual members of the CAC are described in this section. It also outlines procedures for selecting a CAC chair, vice chair, and secretary and describes the responsibilities of each of these positions.

5. *Organization*

This section describes local government's role in providing basic orientation for CAC members and CAC members' responsibility to attend orientation sessions. If resources are budgeted for CAC work, this section explains what compensation and expenses are allowable. Where applicable, it also describes members' responsibilities to uphold confidentiality statements and agreements.

6. *Meetings*

This section describes the procedures to be followed in meetings and explains that all local government CACs must operate in accordance with the North Carolina General Statutes' open meetings law. It specifies what types of meetings (for example, special, emergency, teleconference, etc.) are allowed and who may call those meetings. This section also sets forth what records (for example, meeting minutes, reports, etc.) the CAC must keep and how it will inform the local governing board of its progress, actions, and recommendations.

7. *Subcommittees*

In this section, the policy states whether the CAC has the authority to establish its own subcommittees. If the local governing board grants that authority, this section clarifies for what purposes subcommittees may be formed, what process will be used to form subcommittees, what membership criteria apply, and what operating standards shall be used.

8. *Quorum*

This section establishes the minimum number of voting members required to constitute a quorum. If necessary, this section clarifies what standards apply to quorums for statutory and optional CACs.

9. *Voting*

This section addresses who is allowed or required to vote and what kinds of votes (for example, proxy, ex officio, etc.) are permissible.

10. *Authorized Spokespersons*

This section designates the authorized spokespersons for the CAC and delineates to whom, under what circumstances, and how such authority may be delegated.

11. *Conflict of Interest*

This section describes relevant state laws and local policies concerning conflict of interest and assures CAC members access to local government legal counsel. It also outlines the process by which citizens can question whether a CAC member has a conflict of interest.

12. *Compensation and Travel Reimbursement*

If the local government offers compensation and/or travel reimbursements to CAC members, details of how reimbursements are to be approved and processed appear in this section.

13. *Limitation of Powers*

This section makes clear that CAC members are not authorized by the local governing board to operate outside the scope of this document. It also gives the local governing board authority to address noncompliance issues.

Conclusion

Apart from public hearings, citizen advisory committees are the most frequent way that local governments engage people in local decisions. Citizen advisory committees can be structured in a variety of ways to serve many different purposes. Local elected and appointed leaders should carefully consider their reasons for establishing CACs and structure the process so that committees have the right people and tools to carry out assigned tasks. Local governments have many options when creating CACs, but using a standard policy framework can clarify CAC members' roles and CACs' responsibilities. Good governance at the local level often depends upon gaining the trust and commitment of community stakeholders. CACs are one way that local governments can increase the transparency of their work and involve citizens directly in the democratic process.

Appendix A: Sample Tracking Chart for Citizen Advisory Committees

CAC name/Annual appointment date	Current members (by seat if appropriate)	Contact info	Appointed on	Seat expires	Eligible for reappointment	Notes
Board of Health/ Appointments made annually on June 1	County Commissioner: Ms. Jane Smith	44 Smith Way Troutland, NC 28888 e-mail: jsmith@gmail.com (H) 444-5511 (M) 445-2345	June 1, 2009	June 1, 2010	N/A	Commissioner Smith has been on the Public Health Board for two years.
	Physician: Dr. Dave Jones	4 Jones Loop Road Fish, NC 28889 e-mail: docjones@gmail.com (H) 444-9111 (M) 445-4357	June 1, 2009	June 1, 2012	Yes	First term
	Pharmacist: Mr. Phil Pillar	404 Shop Street Troutland, NC 28888 e-mail: philpill@gmail.com (H) 444-1122 (M) 445-5555	June 1, 2002 June 1, 2005 June 1, 2008	June 1, 2005 June 1, 2008 June 1, 2011	No	Third term
	Veterinarian: Dr. Charles Perdue	707 Hounds Way Bobbin, NC 28887 e-mail: clp@gmail.com (H) 446-2321 (M) 457-5334	June 1, 2002 June 1, 2005 June 1, 2008	June 1, 2005 June 1, 2008 June 1, 2011	No	Third term
	Optometrist: Dr. Eva Lashing	2020 Seething Way Troutland, NC 28888 e-mail: elash@gmail.com (H) 444-8899 (M) 447-5454	June 1, 2002 June 1, 2005 June 1, 2008	June 1, 2005 June 1, 2008 June 1, 2011	No	Third term
	Dentist: Dr. Penny Crowne	230 Cap St. Troutland, NC 28888 e-mail: pennyc@gmail.com (H) 444-6789 (M) 445-0909	June 1, 2009	June 1, 2012	Yes	First term
	Public Engineer: Ms. Tonya Steel	99 Strong Circle Bobbin , NC 28887 e-mail: tsteel@gmail.com (H) 446-3456 (M) 445-2665	June 1, 2007 June 1, 2010	June 1, 2010 June 1, 2013	Yes	Second term
	Registered Nurse: Mr. Joseph Carer	484 Smith Way Troutland, NC 28888 e-mail: carer@gmail.com (H) 444-3334 (M) 445-6789	June 1, 2007 June 1, 2010	June 1, 2010 June 1, 2013	Yes	Second term
	Public: Mr. John Doe	101 Old Time Drive Fish, NC 28889 e-mail: (H) 444-0008 (M) 444-0099	June 1, 2007 June 1, 2010	June 1, 2010 June 1, 2013	Yes	Second term
	Public: Ms. Donna High	123 Happy Lane Troutland, NC 28888 e-mail: dhigh@gmail.com (H) 444-6835 (M) 445-9797	June 1, 2009	June 1, 2012	Yes	First term
	Public: Vacant					

IAP2 Spectrum
of Public Participation

iap2
International Association
for Public Participation

Increasing Level of Public Impact →

	Inform	**Consult**	**Involve**	**Collaborate**	**Empower**
Public participation goal	To provide the public with balanced and objective information to assist them in understanding the problem, alternatives, opportunities and/or solutions.	To obtain public feedback on analysis, alternatives and/or decisions.	To work directly with the public throughout the process to ensure that public concerns and aspirations are consistently understood and considered.	To partner with the public in each aspect of the decision including the development of alternatives and the identification of the preferred solution.	To place final decision-making in the hands of the public.
Promise to the public	We will keep you informed.	We will keep you informed, listen to and acknowledge concerns and aspirations, and provide feedback on how public input influenced the decision.	We will work with you to ensure that your concerns and aspirations are directly reflected in the alternatives developed and provide feedback on how public input influenced the decision.	We will look to you for advice and innovation in formulating solutions and incorporate your advice and recommendations into the decisions to the maximum extent possible.	We will implement what you decide.
Example techniques	▪ Fact sheets ▪ Web sites ▪ Open houses	▪ Public comment ▪ Focus groups ▪ Surveys ▪ Public meetings	▪ Workshops ▪ Deliberative polling	▪ Citizen advisory committees ▪ Consensus-building ▪ Participatory decision-making	▪ Citizen juries ▪ Ballots ▪ Delegated decision

Appendix C: Citizen Advisory Committee Selection Matrix

The purpose of the CAC is _____

Candidates' Characteristics

Candidate's Role in Community	Age <20	Age 21–40	Age 41–65	Age 65+	Gender Female	Gender Male	Years of Residence <5	Years of Residence 6–10	Years of Residence 11+	Race/Ethnicity African American	Race/Ethnicity Caucasian	Race/Ethnicity Hispanic	Race/Ethnicity Other	Education <High School	Education High School	Associate's Degree	Bachelor's Degree	Graduate or Professional Degree	Resources Money	Resources Network	Resources Equipment	Resources Other	Interest High	Interest Medium	Interest Low	Vision Yes	Vision No	Compatible Yes	Compatible No
Elected official																													
Business owner																													
Professional (e.g., law, medicine, finance)																													
Represents civic organization																													
Represents faith community																													
Represents neighborhood association																													
Represents educational community (e.g., K–12, community college, university)																													
Other																													
TOTAL																													

Appendix D: Model CAC Policy Template

1. *Scope*

PURPOSE:
To establish policy and procedure whereby the _____ County/City governing board will make appointments to _____ County/City public advisory boards, committees, commissions, and councils (hereinafter referred to as "citizen advisory committees").

The _____ County/City governing board may appoint a citizen advisory committee whose duty is to serve in an advisory capacity to _____ concerning _____ .

Note: A clear purpose should be included in every policy that establishes a CAC.

AUTHORITY:
The _____ County/City governing board may establish rules and regulations in reference to managing the interest and business of the County/City. For statutory boards, authority may include reference to applicable General Statutes.

The County/City governing board has the responsibility to appoint citizens to serve as members of citizen advisory committees established by the board.

County/City department heads and staff are responsible for providing support to the County/City citizen advisory committees.

POLICY:
This policy establishes the parameters for appointments to state-mandated, regional, and/or County/City–developed citizen advisory committees.

PERIODIC REVIEW:
Periodic review of this policy will be conducted every _____ years by the County/City governing board.

Note: This section on the scope of CACs could be included in a generic policy that recognizes the authority of the governing board to establish CACs for any lawful purpose.

2. *Duties*

The _____ citizen advisory committee advises the _____ in the areas of
_____ .

The citizen advisory committee is expected to achieve the following goals: _____ .

The committee must submit final recommendations to the County/City governing board by _____ (date).

The citizen advisory committee, through its membership and subcommittees, maintains continual contact with representative professional groups, stakeholder groups, and industry organizations. In this manner, the citizen advisory committee is kept apprised of current information related to all matters under the jurisdiction of _____ County/City.

All actions of the committee shall be transmitted in writing, on a regular basis, to the County/City [governing board, manager, department director].

Note: Each CAC needs to have specific duties unique to that CAC.

3. Membership

For purposes of consistency, all appointments to _____ citizen advisory committee will be made by the _____ . In order to qualify for an appointment to the _____ _____ citizen advisory committee, a person must meet the following requirements:

  a. All committee members must meet the qualifications for the specific citizen advisory committee or the statutory requirements for an appointed position.
  b. All committee members must eighteen (18) years of age or older unless applying under a youth-designated position.
  c. All committee members shall be permanent residents of the County/City or own real property or work or maintain a place of business in the County/City and shall have good reputations for integrity and community service and shall not have been convicted of or received a deferred sentence for a felony crime.
  d. No nominee to the committee, nor any members of the nominee's immediate family, shall be currently employed by the County/City.
  e. No nominee may currently be a party to nor a legal representative in litigation against the County/City.
  f. Each nominee must be prepared and committed to participating in CAC work in a manner that enhances relationships between the County/City and the community.
  g. Citizen advisory committee members serve the people of _____ County/City. As such, their role includes their commitment for full participation in the citizen advisory committee's meetings and activities.

EXCEPTIONS:

The County/City governing board may waive requirements, with the exception of statutory requirements.

Note: A local government may choose to adopt a generic policy regarding the membership qualifications for all CACs.

COMPOSITION:

  a. The County/City _____ shall appoint all voting members to the _____ _____ citizen advisory committee. The voting members shall reflect the cultural and ethnic diversity of the community.

b. The _____ advisory committee shall be composed of _____ voting members and _____ nonvoting members. The _____ County/City department's representative shall serve as the nonvoting member of the committee.

c. _____ members appointed by the _____ County/City shall represent the following [demographic characteristics, geographic regions, professional disciplines, etc.].

d. Up to _____ ex officio members appointed by the _____ serve until appointment of their successors by the _____ .

Note: The composition of CACs may vary according to their purpose. The makeup of the CAC should be included in each CAC policy.

SELECTION CRITERIA:

Appointed members, except for the appointed ex officio members, shall be qualified by _____ _____ . They shall be appointed from nominees recommended by _____ , whose applications were submitted to _____ by _____ (date), or designated representative of _____ .

APPOINTMENT:

a. All members of citizen advisory boards serve at the pleasure of the _____ County/City governing board.

b. Appointments to citizen advisory boards will be initiated with a public application process, and recommendations from _____ , and/or nominations by [community and/or professional organizations].

c. All appointments to advisory boards will be made by _____ County/City governing board by _____ (date).

d. No person appointed to a _____ County/City citizen advisory committee shall serve on that board for more than _____ terms or more than a period of _____ years, whichever is longer.

e. Extension of a member's term may be approved by the County/City governing board if it is determined that it is in the best interest of the County/City to allow an individual to continue to serve.

Note: Selection could be standardized for all CACs and this section could go in a generic policy.

TERMS:

a. Each appointed citizen advisory committee member shall serve a term of _____ years and hold office until the qualification and appointment of his or her successor or until one year has elapsed since the expiration of the term for which the citizen was appointed, whichever first occurs. No person shall serve as an appointed member of the citizen advisory committee for more than _____ consecutive terms.

b. In order to establish staggered terms, one-third of the original voting members of the citizen advisory committee shall be appointed as follows: three for a one-year term, three for a two-year term, and three for a three-year term. Thereafter, each new voting member shall serve for a three-year term. No voting member shall serve more than _____ term(s).

c. Citizen advisory committee members whose terms are due to expire may request or be asked to accept reappointment to the position.

Note: Local officials may elect not to have term limits for some CACs (e.g., airport authority) when it is difficult to identify, recruit, and keep knowledgeable CAC members.

RESIGNATION:

a. A member of a citizen advisory board shall submit his or her resignation in writing to the Chair of the advisory board on which he or she serves, noting the effective date of the resignation.

b. The Chair will forward a copy of the resignation to the director of the County/City department and to the County/City governing board.

c. The County/City governing board shall recognize the individual's service via a letter or certificate.

d. An announcement of the open seat will be made at the time the resignation becomes effective.

Note: The process for resignations may be included in a generic policy.

VACANCIES:

Upon expiration of the term of service of members or should a vacancy otherwise occur, the _____ County/City [citizen advisory committee, department, governing board] shall have the responsibility of selecting and appointing new members to the committee.

REMOVAL:

a. Members of the _____ County/City citizen advisory committee are expected to exhibit the highest ethical and professional standards. The County/City governing board or designee may remove a member upon a majority vote of the County/City governing board.

b. The County/City governing board may remove any member of the citizen advisory committee for neglect of duty, nonparticipation (defined as missing _____ meetings within _____ months), or other just cause.

RELEASE FROM SERVICE:

a. When it is deemed necessary to release a member from his or her term of appointment on a citizen advisory committee, the affected individual shall be notified by letter.

b. When a citizen advisory committee has completed its function, the members shall be informed of the termination of the citizen advisory committee by letter or e-mail from the County/City governing board and/or the responsible department.

Note: Except where appointment to and removal from statutory boards is established by state law, this section could be part of a generic policy.

4. *Roles and Responsibilities*

MEMBERS:

 a. Members shall attend meetings of the citizen advisory committee, serve on subcommittees, and perform other functions as assigned by the citizen advisory committee chair. For quorum considerations, if a member is unable to attend citizen advisory committee meetings, the member shall contact the [Chair or designated staff] as soon as possible, and at least forty-eight (48) hours before the scheduled meeting.

 b. Ex officio members may be appointed by the _____ County/City [governing board, department] for the purpose of meeting subject-matter expert needs. Ex officio members are nonvoting members of the CAC.

 c. Upon review of the above matters, the _____ County/City citizen advisory committee shall address recommendations and concerns, if any, to the [County/City governing board, department director] in writing.

GOVERNING BOARD:

 a. The _____ County/City [governing board, department] will consider the citizen advisory committee's recommendations or concerns.

 b. Should any concerns remain unresolved after a response has been received from the _____ _____ , the County/City governing board may request that the matter be referred to the County/City [manager, department head].

 c. To enhance trust between the _____ County/City department and the community, members of the citizen advisory committee will:

 1. Assist staff of the _____ County/City department in achieving a greater understanding of the nature and causes of community issues, with an emphasis on improving relations between the department and the citizens.

 2. Recommend methods to encourage and develop the CAC.

 3. Work throughout the community to gain relevant information about CAC issues and communicate these with the County/City governing board and employees.

 4. Promote public awareness of contemporary issues the _____ County/City department must address.

CHAIR, VICE CHAIR, AND SECRETARY SELECTION AND RESPONSIBILITIES:

The Chair of the citizen advisory committee is [nominated, appointed, elected] by the County/City [governing board, department, members of the citizen advisory committee].

Advisory committee Chair and Vice Chair shall be appointed members with at least [one, two] years remaining of their [three-year, four-year] terms.

The Chair and Vice Chair shall serve no more than _____ consecutive terms.

The Chair and the Vice Chair shall assume office on _____ . At the first citizen advisory committee meeting upon assuming office, the citizen advisory committee Chair shall present members with a copy of the citizen advisory committee's charge, scope, and membership.

a. The Committee Chair has the following duties:
   1. Calls all meetings.
   2. Serves as presiding officer.
   3. Assists staff in developing the committee meeting agenda.
   4. Designates subcommittees (unless prohibited by the County/City governing board).
   5. Dissolves or appoints additional subcommittees (subject to committee and/or _____ approval).
   6. Appoints subcommittee chairs and members.
   7. Works in consultation with the _____ .
   8. Carries out citizen advisory committee assignments as required by the _____ .
   9. Designates a Vice Chair for the committee.
   10. Conducts citizen advisory committee meetings and presents a report of the proceedings and resulting motions for approval at _____ County/City governing board meetings.
   11. Reviews all committee minutes and proposed recommendations or assigns another member of the committee to do so.
b. The committee Vice Chair has the following duty:
   1. Presides at citizen advisory committee meetings in the absence of the Chair.
c. The committee Secretary has the following duties:
   1. Takes (or oversees the taking of) minutes for all CAC meetings.
   2. Submits minutes to the Chair (or designated person) to be distributed to CAC members in advance of CAC meetings.
   3. Submits approved CAC minutes to the County/City governing board.
   4. Assures that other records of the CAC are kept as directed by _____ .

Note: Roles and responsibilities are likely to vary by CAC, though some expectations for CAC Chairs and members could be generic.

5. Organization

ORIENTATION AND TRAINING:

The County/City will make available for citizen advisory committee members and department staff periodic training on state and County/City goals and priorities as well as relevant statutes and policies, including open meetings, public records, conflicts of interest, and ethics.

   a. Each member shall attend an orientation presented by the _____ County/City department to familiarize the citizen advisory committee members with the operation of County/City government, the _____ department, and the rules and operating procedures of the citizen advisory committee.
   b. Each voting member will be encouraged to complete the orientation within _____ [weeks, months] of his or her appointment and participate in at least one [ride-along, site visit, training session].

c. Citizen advisory committee members will be issued a _____ manual and should become familiar with its contents.

Note: Some jurisdictions offer a standard orientation for CAC members. In that case, this section could go in a generic policy.

OPERATING EXPENSES:
a. Voting members of the _____ advisory committee are not employees of the County/City.
b. Voting members serve in a voluntary capacity and shall receive *no*/$ ____ monetary compensation nor any other financial or employee benefit from the County/City.
c. The County/City will provide office supplies and assume responsibility for other expenses necessary for the operation of the committee.

Note: Unless CAC members receive different levels of compensation, this section could be included in a generic policy.

CONFIDENTIALITY:
The Chair shall serve as the spokesperson for the citizen advisory committee.

Except for the Chair, no member of the citizen advisory committee shall make any written or oral statement of any confidential matter to any individual or body. A violation will result in immediate removal from the committee.

Members of the citizen advisory committee may receive information regarding personnel matters and other information of a sensitive or confidential nature. It shall be the duty and responsibility of each member to respect and maintain the confidentiality of client issues presented before the board. Neither the citizen advisory committee nor any individual member shall disseminate confidential information received during citizen advisory committee meetings. Citizen advisory committee members are required to sign confidentiality statements and will be removed from the citizen advisory committee upon violation of the confidentiality agreement.

Note: A standard for confidentiality across all CACs should be included in a generic policy.

6. Meetings

In accordance with the North Carolina General Statutes, all meetings are open to the public as required by the open meetings act.

Unless otherwise specified, public meetings will follow the standard rules of procedure defined by the County/City governing board. The members of the citizen advisory committee shall adopt other rules and procedures relating to the operation of the committee as needed. The citizen advisory committee members shall determine the date, time, and place for each meeting.
a. Regular Citizen Advisory Committee and Subcommittee Meetings
   The citizen advisory committee convenes upon call of the Chair and usually meets on a [weekly, monthly, quarterly] basis. The meetings may be held in [specified or various locations] within

the County/City. Subcommittee meeting dates shall be set by the subcommittee Chairs and shall be scheduled in conjunction with citizen advisory committee meetings.

b. Special Meetings

A majority of citizen advisory committee members or the Chair may call special meetings at any time for any specific business. Special meetings, such as appeals, are convened at a location selected by the Chair.

c. Meetings Held via Teleconference

Teleconference meetings shall be held only in unusual circumstances and shall not replace regularly scheduled committee meetings. No regular meeting or appeal hearing shall be conducted via teleconference. Under no circumstances should a teleconference meeting exceed [one hour].

d. Emergency Meetings

A majority of citizen advisory committee members or the Chair may call a meeting in emergency circumstances by providing telephone notice to media outlets at least one hour prior to the meeting. An emergency situation includes a disaster that severely impairs the public's health or safety. In the event telephone services are not working, notice that the meeting occurred must be given as soon as possible after the meeting.

e. Meeting Notices

Notice of public citizen advisory committee meetings (including appeal hearings) and agendas shall be made available to all members and interested parties, and to any person who so requests, at least ten (10) days in advance of the meeting by e-mail and by posting on the _____ website.

f. Agendas

A. Committee Chairs (and/or CAC members) should submit agenda items to the _____ _____ (designated person) at least _____ days prior to a scheduled meeting.

B. The agenda must provide a description of each item of business to be transacted or discussed so that interested members of the public will be capable of understanding the nature of each agenda item.

C. As a general rule, only those items appearing on the agenda will be discussed or voted on. However, if an item is raised by a member of the public, the citizen advisory committee may accept testimony and discuss the item so long as no action is taken until a subsequent meeting.

D. With the Chair's agreement, the designated staff will develop and distribute to each member an agenda listing the matters to be considered at upcoming citizen advisory committee meetings. Also, so far as practicable, copies of all written reports that are to be presented to the citizen advisory committee for members' review will be included in this package at least ten (10) days before the meeting.

g. Minutes

Minutes shall be taken of all citizen advisory committee meetings and submitted to the County/City [governing board, clerk, department head] for consideration and approval.

h. All recommendations and reports of the citizen advisory committee, approved in the form of motions, shall be conveyed exclusively to the County/City governing board for action. Approved motions are forwarded to the County/City governing board for consideration, approval, or denial. Outcomes are reported back to the citizen advisory committee.

7. Subcommittees

a. Subcommittees [may/may not be] formed by the citizen advisory committee to research and make recommendation on special issues or areas in order to carry out the duties of the _____ citizen advisory committee. All subcommittees shall be reviewed on an annual basis to determine continued need and realignment with the priorities of the citizen advisory committee.

b. Except as approved by the [County/City governing board, manager, or department head], the majority of members of a subcommittee shall be _____ County/City residents.

c. Subcommittees are ad hoc and temporary in nature. Approved ad hoc subcommittees must have documented goals, deliverables, and a timeline, and the subcommittee will cease to meet when these are satisfied.

d. The citizen advisory committee Chair may request that the County/City governing board change the structure and/or operating procedures of the citizen advisory committee if he or she deems it essential for improving the committee's productivity and effectiveness.

e. Subcommittee Formation and Operation:

  a. Formation

  A subcommittee can be formed with the approval of the County/City [governing board, manager, department head].

  b. Operation

  Subcommittees shall operate as specified.

    A. A member of the subcommittee shall take responsibility for assigning a note taker and for reporting to the full citizen advisory committee the subcommittee's progress toward its stated objectives, including dissenting view points.

    B. Subcommittees shall operate by [consensus or majority vote].

    C. Subcommittees may request a technical representative, to be approved by the County/City [governing board, manager, department head].

    D. _____ will support necessary and reasonable accommodations for subcommittee members, such as teleconferencing for someone who cannot physically attend due to disability. (Members can submit their requests for accommodation in writing by mail or e-mail to _____ staff.)

    E. Subcommittees shall operate openly as defined by state laws and local policies.

      a. Membership

      Membership on subcommittees shall be voluntary unless policy dictates otherwise.

8. Quorum

A quorum for a meeting of citizen advisory committees shall consist of one more than half the voting members.

9. *Voting*

Decisions are reached by a simple majority vote unless otherwise required by law. All voting will be conducted in open meetings, except when in closed session as defined in the open meetings law. No issues can be voted upon unless a quorum is present.

    a. Citizen Advisory Committee Meetings

        Only appointed members can vote at advisory committee meetings. Appointed members shall not delegate their vote to another member.

        Advisory committee members and others appointed by the _____ County/City governing board may vote at citizen advisory committee meetings.

    b. Voting by Chairs

        The Chair of the advisory committee [may/may not] participate and vote on all issues.

    c. Proxy

        Voting by proxy is not allowed.

    d. Ex Officio

        Individuals appointed as ex officio members of the CAC are not allowed to vote.

10. *Authorized Spokespersons*

The advisory committee Chair and County/City department director are authorized spokespersons for the advisory committee. Other committee members may speak on behalf of the advisory committee only upon authorization by the Chair or County/City _____ department director.

11. *Conflict of Interest*

During citizen advisory committee meetings, a member shall abstain from voting when he or she has a conflict of interest as defined by the County/City governing board's policy.

During review proceedings, the applicant has the right to question the conflict of interest of any voting member. The citizen advisory committee Chair should consult with the County/City attorney on any potential conflict in appeal matters.

Note: Conflict of interest is likely to be uniform for all CACs; thus this section could be covered in a generic policy.

12. *Compensation and Travel Reimbursement*

    a. Appointed advisory committee members shall receive *no*/$ _____ compensation for their services.

    b. Eligibility for Reimbursement of Travel Expenses

        1. The Chair shall, to the extent practicable, schedule hearings and citizen advisory committee meetings to minimize travel and per diem costs.

        2. Payment of expenses to citizen advisory committee members shall occur only when travel has been approved prior to the time the expenses are incurred.

3. [County/City manager, department head, finance officer] shall reimburse authorized reasonable and necessary travel and incidental business expenses to individuals who perform services as appointed members of the citizen advisory committee. Only citizen advisory committee members who attend meetings as part of their duties shall have their expenses reimbursed.
4. Citizen advisory committee members shall be reimbursed in accordance with current local and/or state rules and regulations. Expense claims shall be submitted as required in _____ County/City travel procedures.
5. Transportation expense claims shall include charges essential for transportation to and from the meeting place. Reimbursement shall be made only for the local government's standard mileage allowance. Travel should be via the shortest, most commonly traveled route.

Note: Travel policies may be applied equally to all CACs. In that case, this section could go in a generic policy.

13. *Limitation of Powers*

Compliance with statutes and ordinances:

Nothing contained in this statement of policy and procedures shall be construed to be in conflict with any state law or _____ County/City ordinance. Should there be an appearance of conflict, the appropriate state law or County/City ordinance shall prevail.

Neither the citizen advisory committee, nor any member thereof, shall:
1. Incur County/City expense or obligate the County/City in any manner.
2. Release any written or oral report of any board activity to any individual or body other than the _____ or the Office of the County/City Manager. The committee Chair may issue a press release after consultation with the [department head or County/City manager].
3. Independently investigate citizen complaints against the _____ County/City department or an employee of the department.
4. Conduct any activity that might constitute or be construed as an official governmental review of departmental or employee actions.
5. Conduct any activity that might constitute or be construed as establishment of County/City or department policy.
6. Violate the confidentiality of any information related to matters involving pending or forthcoming civil or criminal litigation.

Matters pertaining to discipline will be the sole responsibility of the _____ County/City governing board and not the citizen advisory committee. The activities of the citizen advisory committee shall, at all times, be conducted in accordance with all federal, state, and local laws.

Note: The city or county is ultimately responsible for the actions of CACs. Therefore, a statement limiting CAC powers could be in a generic policy.

Suggested Reading

Bell, A. Fleming, II. *Ethics, Conflicts, and Offices: A Guide for Local Officials.* 2nd ed. Chapel Hill, NC: UNC School of Government, 2010.

Bluestein, Frayda. "Article 20: Contracts, Competitive Bidding, and Conflicts of Interest." In *County and Municipal Government in North Carolina.* Chapel Hill, NC: UNC School of Government, 2007.

Lawrence, David M. *Open Meetings and Local Governments in North Carolina: Some Questions and Answers.* 7th ed. Chapel Hill, NC: UNC School of Government, 2008.

Lawrence, David M. *Public Records Law for North Carolina Local Governments.* 2nd ed. Chapel Hill, NC: UNC School of Government, 2009.

North Carolina General Statutes § 14-234. Public officers or employees benefiting from public contracts; exceptions. *Available at* ncleg.net.

North Carolina General Statutes § 14-234.1. Misuse of confidential information. *Available at* ncleg.net.

North Carolina General Statutes § 133-32. Gifts and favors regulated. *Available at* ncleg.net.

Notes

1. See Maureen Berner, "Citizen Participation in Local Government Budgeting," *Popular Government* 66, no. 3 (Spring 2001): 23–30; Kaifeng Yang and Kathe Callahan, "Citizen Involvement Efforts and Bureaucratic Responsiveness: Participatory Values, Stakeholder Pressures and Administrative Practicality," *Public Administration Review* 67, no. 2 (Mar. 2007): 249–64, *available at* http://soc.kuleuven.be/io/performance/paper/WS4/WS4_Kathe%20Callahan.pdf (accessed Aug. 30, 2010).

2. Pamela D. Gibson, Donald P. Lacy, and Michael J. Dougherty, "Improving Performance and Accountability in Local Government with Citizen Participation," *Innovation Journal: The Public Sector Innovation Journal* 10, no. 1 (2005), *available at* www.innovation.cc/volumes-issues/gibson1.pdf (accessed Aug. 30, 2010).

3. Lisa Blomgren Bingham, Tina Nabatchi, and Rosemary O'Leary, "The New Governance: Practices and Processes for Stakeholder and Citizen Participation in the Work of Government," *Public Administration Review* 65, no. 5 (Sept./Oct. 2005).

4. Jill D. Moore, "Article 41: Public Health," in *County and Municipal Government in North Carolina* (UNC School of Government, 2007).

5. Janet Mason, "Article 42: Social Services," in *County and Municipal Government in North Carolina* (UNC School of Government, 2007).

6. Mark Botts, "Article 44: Mental Health," in *County and Municipal Government in North Carolina* (UNC School of Government, 2007).

7. R. Irvin and J. Stansbury, "Citizen Participation in Decision Making: Is It Worth the Effort?" *Public Administration Review* 64, no. 1 (Jan./Feb. 2004).

8. Bingham, Nabatchi, and O'Leary, "The New Governance."

9. Tanya Heikkila and Kimberley Roussin Isett, "Citizen Involvement and Performance Management in Special-Purpose Governments," *Public Administration Review* 67, no. 2 (Mar. 2007).

10. Irvin and Stansbury, "Citizen Participation in Decision Making."

11. Irvin and Stansbury, "Citizen Participation in Decision Making."

12. Esther Prins, "The Challenges of Fostering Community Participation: A Case Study of a Community-Based Organization in Rural California," *Journal of the Community Development Society* 36, no. 2 (2005).

13. James Meadowcroft, "Deliberative Democracy," in *Environmental Governance Reconsidered: Challenges, Choices, and Opportunities,* ed. Robert F. Durant, Daniel J. Fiorino, and Rosemary O'Leary (MIT Press, 2004).

14. See Patrick Bishop and Glyn Davis, "Mapping Public Participation in Policy Choices," *Australian Journal of Public Administration* 61, no. 1 (Mar. 2002): 14–29; Gene Row and Lynn J. Frewer, "A Typology of Public Engagement Mechanisms, *Science, Technology, & Human Values* 30 (2005): 251, *available at* http://sth.sagepub.com/content/30/2/251.full.pdf+html (accessed Aug. 30, 2010).

15. See Bingham, Nabatchi, and O'Leary, "The New Governance"; Gibson, Lacy, and Dougherty, "Improving Performance and Accountability in Local Government with Citizen Participation"; Carol Ebdon and Aimee L. Franklin, "Citizen Participation in Budgeting Theory," *Public Administration Review* 66, no. 3

(May/June 2006); Brandi Koehler and Tomas M. Koontz, "Citizen Participation in Collaborative Watershed Partnerships," *Environmental Management* 41 (2008): 143–54; UNC School of Government, "The Public Intersection Project" (2002), *available at* www.publicintersection.unc.edu.

16. Irvin and Stansbury, "Citizen Participation in Decision Making."

17. Mark B. Brown, "Survey Article: Citizen Panels and the Concept of Representation," *The Journal of Political Philosophy* 14, no. 2 (2006): 203–25; Yang and Callahan, "Citizen Involvement Efforts and Bureaucratic Responsiveness"; Koehler and Koontz "Citizen Participation in Collaborative Watershed Partnerships."

18. Jim Collins, *Good to Great: Why Some Companies Make the Leap . . . and Others Don't* (New York: Harpers Business, 2001).

19. Koehler and Koontz, "Citizen Participation in Collaborative Watershed Partnerships."

20. Gibson, Lacy, and Dougherty, "Improving Performance and Accountability in Local Government with Citizen Participation."

21. Koehler and Koontz, "Citizen Participation in Collaborative Watershed Partnerships."

22. See Prins, "The Challenges of Fostering Community Participation"; Ebdon and Franklin, "Citizen Participation in Budgeting Theory"; Rowe and Frewer, "A Typology of Public Engagement Mechanisms."

23. UNC School of Government, "The Public Intersection Project."